Sep 2016

D1603172

A FIRST LOOK AT AMERICA'S PRESIDENTS

RONALD REAGAN

The 40th President

by Jim Gigliotti

Consultants:
Philip Nash, Associate Professor of History
Pennsylvania State University
Sharon, Pennsylvania

Soo Chun Lu, Associate Professor of History
Indiana University of Pennsylvania
Indiana, Pennsylvania

BEARPORT
PUBLISHING

New York, New York

Credits

Cover, Courtesy Ronald Reagan Presidential Library; 4, © A.F. Archive/Alamy Stock Photo; 5, Courtesy Ronald Reagan Presidential Library; 6, Courtesy Ronald Reagan Presidential Library; 7T, Courtesy Ronald Reagan Presidential Library; 7B, Courtesy Ronald Reagan Presidential Library; 8L, © OSORIOarists/Shutterstock; 8R, Courtesy Ronald Reagan Presidential Library; 9, Courtesy Ronald Reagan Presidential Library; 10L, Courtesy Ronald Reagan Presidential Library; 10R, Richard Thomas/Dreamstime; 11T, Courtesy Ronald Reagan Presidential Library; 11B, Courtesy Ronald Reagan Presidential Library; 12, Courtesy Ronald Reagan Presidential Library; 13, Courtesy Ronald Reagan Presidential Library; 13TR, © OldPoliticals.com; 14, Courtesy Ronald Reagan Presidential Library; 15T, Courtesy Ronald Reagan Presidential Library; 15B, Courtesy Ronald Reagan Presidential Library; 16, Courtesy U.S. Air Force; 17, Courtesy Ronald Reagan Presidential Library; 18, Courtesy Ronald Reagan Presidential Library; 19, Courtesy Ronald Reagan Presidential Library; 20T, Courtesy Ronald Reagan Presidential Library; 20B, Courtesy Ronald Reagan Presidential Library; 21TL, © OldPoliticals.com; 21TR, Courtesy Ronald Reagan Presidential Library; 21B, Courtesy Ronald Reagan Presidential Library; 22, Courtesy Architect of the Capitol.

Publisher: Kenn Goin
Senior Editor: Joyce Tavolacci
Creative Director: Spencer Brinker
Production and Photo Research: Shoreline Publishing Group LLC

Library of Congress Cataloging-in-Publication Data

Names: Gigliotti, Jim, author.
Title: Ronald Reagan: the 40th President / by Jim Gigliotti.
Description: New York, New York : Bearport Publishing, [2017] | Series: A
   first look at America's presidents | Audience: Ages 6–10._ | Includes
   bibliographical references and index.
Identifiers: LCCN 2016012115 (print) | LCCN 2016012662 (ebook) | ISBN
   9781944102692 (library binding) | ISBN 9781944997366 (ebook)
Subjects: LCSH: Reagan, Ronald—Juvenile literature. | United
   States—Politics and government—1981–1989—Juvenile literature. |
   Presidents—United States—Biography—Juvenile literature.
Classification: LCC E877 .G55 2017 (print) | LCC E877 (ebook) | DDC
   973.927092—dc23
LC record available at http://lccn.loc.gov/2016012115

For more information, write to Bearport Publishing Company, Inc., 45 West 21st Street, Suite 3B, New York, New York 10010. Printed in the United States of America.

10 9 8 7 6 5 4 3 2 1

CONTENTS

People cheered. A band played. It was November 1980, and Ronald Reagan had just been **elected** president. Reagan looked and spoke just like a movie star. In fact, he had been one! Now he was taking on the biggest role of his life.

Reagan as a young actor

Ronald Reagan was the 40th president. He served from 1981 to 1989.

Young Reagan

Ronald Wilson Reagan was born in Illinois in 1911. He grew up in a small town. As a boy, Ronald was quiet. He loved to read stories about heroes. In his favorite books, the good guys always beat the bad guys.

Ronald

The Reagan family—Ronald's father, mother, and brother, Neil

6

In high school, Ronald played football and basketball.

When Ronald was a child, his father called him Dutch. The nickname stuck.

Ronald

Ronald's high school football team

College Days

Reagan worked hard to save enough money to go to college. There, he studied **economics** and joined the student government. When he was a freshman, he spoke out against cuts to school programs. Reagan learned his words could make a difference.

As a young man, Reagan worked as a lifeguard. He rescued more than 70 people!

In college, Reagan acted in several plays. He loved being on stage.

9

Movie Star

After college, Reagan got a job as a radio **sportscaster**. He still enjoyed acting, however. In 1937, he went to Hollywood, California, and tried out to become an actor. A large movie company hired him! Reagan went on to perform in more than 50 movies.

Reagan's first job was in radio.

The first movie Reagan starred in was called *Love Is on the Air*.

In 1952, Reagan married actress Nancy Davis. They had two children.

On to Politics

While still making movies, Reagan began to focus on **politics**. In 1964, he gave a speech in support of Barry Goldwater, who was running for president. Goldwater lost, but Reagan became a new star in politics. Many people thought he should run for governor of California. In 1966, he did—and won!

Reagan was often called the Great Communicator. Why? He was very good at making speeches.

Reagan (right) giving a speech for Barry Goldwater (left)

Victory! Reagan celebrates his 1966 win.

REAGAN FOR GOVERNOR

13

Tax Cutter

Reagan was a popular governor. After serving for eight years, he decided to try leading the whole country. In 1980, Reagan was elected president. At the time, Americans were struggling to pay their bills. Reagan cut **taxes** so people could keep more of their money.

Reagan and Nancy on the day he became president

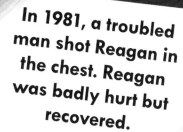

In 1981, a troubled man shot Reagan in the chest. Reagan was badly hurt but recovered.

Reagan waves to a crowd in Washington, DC. Seconds later, he was shot.

In 1984, Reagan was reelected president.

Cold Warrior

When Reagan was president, the United States and the Soviet Union did not trust each other. There was a constant fear that the two countries would go to war. This period was known as the Cold War. In response, Reagan made the U.S. military stronger. He also worked with Soviet leaders to reduce the number of deadly **nuclear weapons**.

A nuclear missile

The Soviet Union was a huge country made up of 15 smaller states, including Russia. It was formed in 1922 and broke apart in 1991.

Reagan worked closely with Soviet leader Mikhail Gorbachev (right).

17

Remembering Reagan

Reagan left office in 1989. He moved to California. Today, Reagan is remembered as a strong and **optimistic** leader. He worked hard to end the Cold War. He also fought to bring hope to Americans during difficult times.

A library was built in California to honor Ronald Reagan.

Reagan at his horse ranch in California

In 2004, Reagan died from Alzheimer's. This disease affects the brain.

TIMELINE

Here are some major events from Ronald Reagan's life.

1911
Ronald Reagan is born in Tampico, Illinois, on February 6.

1932
Reagan graduates from Eureka College.

1910   1920   1930   1940   1950

1937
Reagan appears in his first movie, *Love Is on the Air*.

1952
Reagan marries Nancy Davis.

1981
Reagan is shot and survives.

1966
Reagan is elected governor of California.

1984
Reagan wins a second term as president.

1989
Reagan leaves office.

1960   1970   1980   1990   2000

1980
Reagan runs for president and wins.

2004
Reagan dies on June 5 at the age of 93.

FACTS and QUOTES

Reagan loved jelly beans. He often gave them as gifts to White House visitors.

"Government's first duty is to protect the people, not run their lives."

Reagan was the oldest U.S. president. He was 77 when he left office.

"We can't help everyone, but everyone can help someone."

"There's nothing better for the inside of a man than the outside of a horse."

GLOSSARY

economics (eh-kuh-NOM-iks) the study of the way money, goods, and services are made and used in a society

elected (ih-LEKT-uhd) chosen by voting

nuclear weapons (NOO-klee-ur WEP-uhnz) bombs or missiles that use a kind of energy that can cause a powerful explosion

optimistic (*op*-tuh-MISS-tik) believing that good things will happen

politics (POL-ih-tiks) everything to do with running for and holding public office

sportscaster (SPORTS-kast-ur) someone who gives information about sports or a sports event on radio or television

taxes (TAKS-es) money people pay to support the government

Index

Read More

Milton, Joyce. *Who Was Ronald Reagan?* New York: Grosset & Dunlap (2005).

Sutcliffe, Jane. *Ronald Reagan (History Maker Bios).* Minneapolis, MN: Lerner (2008).

Venezia, Mike. *Ronald Reagan: Fortieth President 1981–1989 (Getting to Know the U.S. Presidents).* New York: Children's Press (2008).

Learn More Online

To learn more about Ronald Reagan, visit
www.bearportpublishing.com/AmericasPresidents

About the Author:
Jim Gigliotti writes books for kids and adults. He lives in Southern California—not too far from the Ronald Reagan Presidential Library in Simi Valley!